Poetic

Justice

Giving justice through the outlet of poetry

Poetic Mumma

Aaron Allen

Copyrights information-

I AM A POET

So, to that
I commit.
Pleas no comment
Just read.
That's commitment.
Read my lines!
Read my script!
And if your tough
Read my lips!
I'm a poet.
Don't you forget it.

LOVE

I Love you.

But you curse me.

I helped you.

And you left me

RAP

From rhythm and blues

To rhythm and poetry

crafted with creativity.

They both are lovely.

UNBREAKABLE CHAINS

Real friends are hard to come by,
When blessed with one always identify,
Cherish the bond, forgive petty mistakes,
A connection between time and distance can't break.

IN THIS WORLD

There are people in this world.
thriving on deception and lies,
Trying to push others down too deep to rise,

There are people in this world.
speaking up for what is true,
Fighting and demanding
when justice is overdue,

There are people in this world.
totally consumed by hate,
Making any moment an opportunity to abuse and discriminate,

There are people in this world.
advocating to make things fair,
Voices for the voiceless silent by their pain and despair,

There are people in this world.
with cruel intentions in their hearts,
Demonstrated evil and destruction fuel motives once the chaos
starts.

I AM POETIC JUSTICE

I write rhymes about my diverse lifetime,

All the injustices and crime,

The mountains I've been made to climb,

Also,

every success HAS been blessed,

Made progress,

beats being oppressed,

Stories causing laughter and tears,

they're situations I've endured over years,

Written books so I can say a poet's one of my careers,

Some have fears for when I write raw honesty appears,

A poet greatly makes up who I am – without, my heart and soul would be in deep arrears.

POCKET LAUNCHER

I am very kind.

but don't mistake it for a second,

When I have said something important that must be said

I mean every word I speak,

My feelings are uniquely authentic.

still, I make other people a priority,

If you push me too far

don't be surprised with everything you will soon see,

Chances to redeem will be offered but I promise you there is a limit,

I don't have space for people who keep assuming I'm in desperate
need to fill it,

I choose who I have in my life, and I will treat you with respect,

But if I'm not mutually respected, I will instantly reject,

When I invest in you, I will go to the very ends of the earth,

No allowances to be used here for I do know of my worth,

It doesn't take a lot to notice when relationships are one sided,

It's not my fault if you believe I am naïve or misguided,

Ensuring complete understanding that the world must obey self -
proclaimed saviors,

I refuse to repeat cycles drenched in violence, delusions, rage and
lies soaked down to the core.

MY DAUGHTER DEAREST

I know now I love you infinitely more than before.

Your presence revealed a love.

Without a shadow of a doubt

you are my entire existence,

The reason I can hold my head up.

standing proud and walking tall

My only reason to never quit or give up on,

Have unlimited persistence,

You are my guiding, eternally glowing light,

My favorite sentimental heart-warming poem to recite,

I'd give my life, everything in a flash for your sake,

Nothing convinces me that good people are real,

The exception is I know you're true,

You radiate joy to my heart like the sight of a rare, magical shade of teal,

No matter what issues life throws at us hand in hand we'll battle through,

Promising forever everything and anything you want or need you can always tell me how you feel.

DEPRESSION REFLECTION

My sky is black with pouring rain,
All night I have felt constant pain,
I don't know what to do or where to turn,
Peace is what I yearn for.

Nothing I do ever seems to be right,
Always at battle and losing the fight,
Wishing that I was not me,
My best never is to be.

Contemplating on my own,
Probably best to isolate alone,
Then I wouldn't bother anyone,
Or darken other people's sun.

I don't feel I'm good enough,
Life is always very rough,
It's not my fault it is this way,
All that I can do is pray.

STEPS

Any sized step towards achieving a goal is an achievement,
Be proud of yourself and recognize the task done,
Remember problems don't come with complete positive treatment,
First steps are where absolutely everyone has begun,
Each time will eventually get you on the other side,
Looking back freely no longer trapped away,
I am living proof it happens so keep trying every day.

SELFISHNESS AND COMPASSION

Hurtful, heartache, hiding, helpless, hell,

Pressure, painful, paper, prayer, pen,

All in unity yet individually too,

Single words put together create power!

Even if there's no interpreting fluently,

Wait! Feel the strength of a pen and a prayer?

Producing that freedom, creative energy, and inner peace,

Releasing relieved emotional damage,

The weight of it all gets less heavy,

Language barriers can be a multitude of things,

I can see clearer now a storm has passed – I'll keep on going,

Finally, I've learned the importance of my own needs.

LEGEND

Legends never die,
A talent no one can deny,
Gifted beyond measure,
An artistic priceless treasure.

TO HEAR THE SOUNDS OF POETRY

My heart explodes from my love for creativity,
Expression becoming bursts of opportunity,
Constructed with emotion laced literacy,
Worn out rhyming dictionary helps consistency.

Inspired by inner demons no need for factionary,
Always seeking forgiveness from Mother Mary,
Reaching deep within to write mindfully,
Visual drumbeats played dead silently.

NOBODY KNOWS

There is so much of me nobody knows,
Like how deeply inside the pain only grows,
And only through rhyme I don't fear that it shows,
Expressing unhealthy highs, complete lows.

I once had strength to push it down and carry on,
For the sake of my child, I dig deep to be strong,
But she only hears about what I do wrong,
I hide from lies made so I don't belong.

Tucked away in my room I sit secluded,
Realistically I am emotionally excluded,
Surrounded by pleasantly ignorant and deluded,
Screaming upon my life they've mentally intruded.

NO MORE

And just like that there was a significant change,

A pounding headache – heart felt strange,

Real talk, I really thought I knew,

There are no exceptions this much is true,

I have never had anger like this,

If only the one of death I'll only kiss,

A blank face and no sign of shame,

Right now, I hate the player and the game,

I don't even want to be around,

The silence is worse than if there were sound,

A tangled web of a liar and a cheat,

Ultimately is what I've come to meet,

There is no more that I can take,

Where do I start when describing this mistake,

Clearly there is no innocent soul,

Dig quickly as I need to dump and fill one more hole.

DEEP WORDS

I spoke deep words to you,
That were all unfortunately true,
What I did not do,
Is think the comments through,
You can't deny what I mean,
The message was blunt but clean,
Taking offence now you have seen,
How for me the situation has been,
It took a word filled attack,
To hopefully have you look back,
Maybe my honesty through a wise crack,
Will help you realize what you lack,
I had no choice but to strike a low blow,
Keeping it real those words I did throw,
Now you sulk and ignore as you go,
My heart just had to tell you so.

DECADES

Friends,

There I was, 26,

Opportunity missed,

I wish I'd said something,

So, we had kissed,

Kept in touch,

Yet did our thing,

Words unsaid,

Both clearly feeling,

Superman came and rescued me,

When with the villain I was dealing,

In the process my heart became his for the taking.

CROSSROAD

My mind is blank, unable to complete a thought,
Emotions running hard like wild horses,
Tears, screams, agony, feeling distraught,
Nothing stops all these powerful forces,
I'm slipping away slowly as I'm curled up on the floor,
Unaware of how long is left until all I know is gone,
I honestly don't know what to do anymore,
This torture is going on for way far too long,
Confined within a toxic room,
Suffocating and I can't find a way out,
Falling on deaf ears are my calls of doom,
Surely the good Lord can hear me shout,
Even though my voice has gone, and all is silent,
No matter what I try and do to make a sound,
Not long before my thoughts could become violent,
And bury my soul deeply into the muddy ground,
I've been at this crossroad many times in the past,
But the right direction to go is always different,
My strength is only just strong enough to last,
And my will to save my sanity nearly spent.

KING OF POETRY

The castle has been captured.

But not me

I had to flee.

Because they wanted my head

They wanted my throne.

Which I was before seated

LUST OR LOVE

Love a poet!

Lust a poet!

For real

Deal or no deal

Deal with the pain

deal with real

Love and lust alike

No matter the cause

They always stay the night.

1988

He decides to talk that year.

I was born that year.

The horse is white.

But this goat is black.

Born in eighty-eight

Born to be a poet.

A POET'S REVELATION

What I saw
Was foresight.
To live the night
To write our spite
There he fell.
A Quiet death
I was I gave him that.
It just seemed right.

BODY PAINT

Her body is a canvas.

I paint her on paper.

This is true poetry.

Her body

alone

I mean.

HATE

There are things I hate.
There are things I love.
When I look at you
Which am I think of

UNMATCHED SKILL

Like I need to say it

Like running it back with this

No time to repeat my lines.

You should already know me.

If not, then

Then this time

Come on, let's match!

To see who's the best line.

SOCIAL JUSTTICE

This just in

A crime again

A usual suspect on the loose

Is it me?

Or is it you?

Is it a he or she?

AMBITIONS AS A WRITER

My only ambition is to write.

To write whatever

Write about the day!

Write about the night!

Write lyrical notes like

A, B, C, D, A

Maybe even write.

What they say

PAYBACK SEEKING YOU

All that was imprisoned in the dark will soon be reaching the light,
Everyday I'm forced to struggle but I won't tap out of the fight,
Severely bruised and bleeding I was ambushed from behind,
My wounds will heal, physical and mental combined,
For I've been given strength to remain on my feet,
As hard as it has been I'll never admit defeat,
A part of me never expected such a win so grand,
With those who love me got my back I took victory by demand.

UNKNOWN KNOWLEDGE

I was shown a deliberate illusion,
Believed my mind created a delusion,
The life that I once swore I knew,
Turned out to be untrue.

Entirety of feelings were based on lies,
Reality becoming a horrid surprise,
Every indicator that I have since learned,
Shows I was undoubtedly destined to be burned.

The thought of every possible sacrifice I had given,
Makes it all impossible to imagine he could ever be forgiven,
But I need to some way for a release within me,
To continue living life emotionally and spiritually free.

ANGELS VS A DEVIL

I can't sleep, continue to think,

Tonight, I was dangerously taken to the brink,

My anger inside burned like a fire,

My mind travelled to many a dark desire,

How can I once have loved who I now know is evil?

Not a single glimmer of hope for goodness to be his retrieval,

Without a second thought he keeps those around him blind,

Complete knowledge of motives to display two frames of mind,

Cowardly liar who doesn't really care he's been exiled,

Pathologically behaves like a golden hearted, innocent child,

Manipulating those who blindly follow all his lies,

Never questioning the endless traits that he denies,

There is an angel on this earth who never fails to make everyone smile,

A soul so beautiful, massive heart it makes my fight for her more worthwhile,

(Next page continue)

I vow to defend her from this devil in her world,

Not stopping till every depraved atrocity is unfurled,

When the day arrives where we will claim the victory,

And brutally expose his entire narcissistic history,

There I'll stand with her both magnificently proud our heads held high,

Her future days lie ahead, and the present consists of not one tear for him to ever cry.

ANGEL ON EARTH

I had the defense of nobody,

Was fighting daily all alone,

Desperately needed somebody,

Surrounded by fire and brimstone,

One day you came along,

Kindly offering me your hand,

Encouraged me not to prolong,

To pull my head out of the sand,

Like an angel on earth,

Appearing to rescue me,

Proclaiming I was of worth,

To those only seeing negativity,

Not once did you leave my side,

Literally on hands and knees to clean,

Together we have cried,

I truly see you as a queen,

Though I conquered at the end,

Your heart remains with me aglow,

With these words all my love I send,

Appreciation that you'll never know.

FLEE

They say things aren't always as they appear,

Deep within I've had a sense of shame and fear,

I try to mask it by wearing a disguise,

Attempting to make it hard to recognize,

I cover the self – loathing and hurt that I feel,

I hope and pray that the time will come when I heal,

It doesn't change what my loved ones receive from me,

It's from myself that I desperately want to flee,

I wonder about others who may be able to relate,

How they deal with being consumed by the hate,

The everyday struggles, the heavy weight to hold,

Going about life with all this hidden and untold.

FALSE PROMISES

Out of the mouth of babes
We hear the lies
Words of wisdom
Talk of wealth
But you
They will not help
Not even a "lil" bit

NEXT GEN

My kids can act
My kids can sing
As talented as they are
They can also even lead

UNCLE AARON

Not worried about another writer
Who thinks he's a spider
Not homophobic
But I am arachnophobia
On the contrary
In role playing games
I can kill them for miles

MY TYPE OF WOMEN (DRINKS)

There are two types of women
I like in this world
Lolitas
And
Ericas
But only after this martini…
Possibly…

MADNESS

I'm mad at him
I can't stand him

But you
You I like

LONG ROAD AHEAD

Left him the long way
Then told the old man to skate
Then continued my journey

LOVING EYES

Her eyes speak of their love without a spoken word,

Past words taken nowhere, like clipped wings on a bird,

The silence so deafening it became all she heard,

A mute cry for help was somewhat more preferred,

She knew that together nothing would be deterred,

Clearly jealousy and anger were being stirred,

Still with pain filled eyes she continued unnerved,

For the love that they have was her ultimate serve.

MENTAL HEALTH

I think I'm ok.

I want to be "GREAT."

Not just "okay"

But I will take it.

Day by day

WE'RE ALL HUMAN

You know those times when you feel totally conflicted?

When logic and emotion intertwine and get all knotted up with each other,

Making it impossible to either untangle or unravel,

Knowing in your mind that it was unfortunately, inevitably irreparable,

Wishing with all your heart that it didn't have to be,

God bestows blessings upon me daily and I am eternally grateful,

I am truly blessed,

I have the amazing Lord Jesus,

Who answered my prayers and gave me my miracle child,

Support from fabulous family and great friends,

Special people who I know will be a part of my future,

I've received gifts and talents that can't be bought with money,

My faith is strong, and I know God has a plan for me,

YOU ARE EMOTIONAL DAMAGE

I am at the point of no return,

You drove me there by force with not a speck of concern,

Degraded and disrespected me now prepare for your turn.

We must do everything the hard way because you never want to learn,

Talking to you is like conversing with a brick wall,

You're ignorant, self-entitled and seek attention, give none,

Fun and games are over, what's next is your life full of turmoil.

Not a soul will come to help you, no matter how loudly you try and call,

I said I would defeat you if my child was played with viciously,

I'm completely done tolerating your rage fueled immaturity,

Open your eyes like an adult so hopefully you clearly see,

No longer wanting you in our lives is a promise I guarantee.

MARRIED TO THE PEN

Holy matrimony

In front of many

Maybe millions

To you my pen

I pronounce my love.

FALSE PROMISES

He told me a lot
He said he would pay me
He said he would give me money
What he really told me
was a lie

WRITE-OHOLIC

Day and night
My pen writer writes
I'm my mind he works
On paper he jerks
Thoughts from cots
That's what they taught

CONFINED

In a in closed space
I raise my ideas to paper
Can't look outside
Just to see if it's later
Been in here so long
That i forgot the time

BLEEDING PEN

Like tears and blood

My pen cries and bleeds

The pain of the loss

Lies within the pens top

It's head cries off

I am her, I am him

Iam the life prying pen

A TEXT MESSAGE

I wander In a land of questions

In this land of wonder

there's are no answers

But I still out a message

Obviously no response

I don't know if they got it

But I can tell I sent it

THEY CRY WOLF

When I'm there

they need me

When I leave

They need me

That's what God told me

NEVERMIND

Pay me no mind

I'm not lying

Don't worry about it

Honestly and truly

I'm fine

Don't worry about me

AS QUIET AS ITS KEPT

We don't speak on these things

No nothing

Nothing at all

No words

No action or verbs

Silence is key

But they all know me

COMING OF AGE

The day and age has come

For you and I

Our times come and go

We all must get old

Our age will show

Only when we grow

LEAVING BEHIND

No more

Leaving behind

No pass

No past

focusing on the future

while I cast my lots

into to future waters

LIFE AS I KNOW IT

It's been going good

Not too bad

It's a little shabby and Shakey.

Nevertheless

I'm still living lively.

COME WITH IT

Come to me

Get close!

Get rough!

Breathe with me

that's close enough.

I don't want to catch anything.

EXTENEDED LIFETIME

More is always better

Because abundance

is what we prefer

IM TIRED

my legs are not doing me any justice

sadly ive overworked them

they are finished

they have walked out from under me

DR. GROY IS NOT A GRIOT

Hes not griot at all

He a villain overall

He doesn't teach

He steals and cheats

He reaches and creeps

Like a old perverted man

He never taught me

He just took lazy peeps

RIGHTFUL AIR

I breathe it rightfully.

As they all can see

The crown of the sky

The breath of the trees

My new thrown awaits

As i move from the old

But in line for the next throne

I patiently wait

THE RIGHT

To know what I know
To say what I say
I feel right in saying.
That that this time
This is my life.

DON'T COME FOR ME

I don't like to talk

I like to act

DIAMONDS IN THE DIRT

As dirty as a kids face

All messy from pursuing greatness

Now I am clean

And enjoying this scene

MAKE RIGHT

Go right

Never left

Leave be the wrong

And pursue the best

JUSTIFICATION

I don't need that identification.

That I have shown

Now please

Let me go on!

A TRUE GRIOT

Mi blood runs mi deep

Like di roots of sugar cane planting

How its planting making mi sweet.

Mi tells the true yard's story.

But mi dirty

Cause from dirt

come living!

OLDER

I'm older.

But adults don't yell.

Right?

But Adults don't kill.

Right?

So, if justice is blind.

Can adults see still?

KING AMAR

He ruled for some time.

But wasn't it's future king?

Now with me coming.

He's trying to get rid of me.

STATUS

For a lot I stand

For women

For men

As they look up to me

I pose for them

But I'm rock solid

And not to be destroyed

DIE FOE

They must go
Maybe not actual death
Maybe just a creative rest

TRIBULATIONS

Hard but good

Put into a cocoon!

But I will grow soon

INSURECTION

Inside jobs

Causes inside purges

They kill their own

For Their own plan

NO JUSTICE

If my own won't do it

Who shall do it ?

A COLORFUL COUNTRY

Don't talk about it

Be it

A NEW LEAF

I'm changing

I'm turning green

Some call it greedy

But it's the new me

I guess my clothes should be matching

Matching my money

IN AND OUT

Came in strong

I should be leaving now

Moving right along

THE LAST POEM

We are here
It's the end
I'm down.

Sorry

I mean I'm done!

(Editing issues)

Until next time... maybe.

MY CONDOLENCES GO OUT TO ALL WHO HAVE LOST LOVED ONES, BE STRONG. IM LIKE YOU, SALUTE.

-AARON ALLEN (Outro)

Made in the USA
Columbia, SC
19 October 2023